The Mahogany Ship

Also by John Egan and published by Ginninderra Press

Lines Continue Forever
The Long Way Home
Crossing the Heads
The Tower
Reworkings (Pocket Poets)
Reworkings 2 (Pocket Poets)
Reworkings 3 (Pocket Poets)
Reworkings 4 (Pocket Poets)
Reworkings 5 (Pocket Poets)
Sydney Central (Pocket Poets)
Play It Louder (Pocket Poets)
Putting to Sea (Pocket Poets)
A Safe Harbour (Pocket Poets)
Visions (Pocket Poets)
Swans (Pocket Poets)
Mischief Eyes (Pocket Poets)
Dreams of Butterflies (Pocket Poets)
Speak to Winter (Pocket Poets)
Red Roses (Pocket Poets)
The Poet and the Painter (Pocket Poets)
Under Pressure (Pocket Poets)
This Here and Now (Picaro Poets)
The Survivor (Picaro Poets)
An Unexpected Harmony (with Brenda Eldridge) (Pocket Poets)
Unknown Edges (with Brenda Eldridge) (Pocket Poets)
Landscapes of the Heart (with Colleen Keating) (Picaro Poets)

John Egan

The Mahogany Ship

For all mariners, for all explorers on the sea, on land, in space, past, present and future

The Mahogany Ship
ISBN 978 1 76041 756 7
Copyright © text John Egan 2019
Cover: RicSou (Shutterstock)
Author photo: Peter Egan

First published 2019 by
GINNINDERRA PRESS
PO Box 3461 Port Adelaide 5015 Australia
www.ginninderrapress.com.au

The long blue rollers of the Southern Ocean
had washed away the outlines of my dream.
Over a sunken world forever lost
the keels of navigators crossed and re-crossed,
and history was shaped to a new theme.

James McAuley, *Captain Quiros*

All you have done was good. Be not downcast,
Or cloud your heart with scruple. God will approve
the work you have pursued with burning love,
and all shall be made perfect at the last.

James McAuley, *Captain Quiros*

1

This visitor
from the mind's confusion
of mist and fog,
this Flying Dutchman
beyond remembered tales,
tacks away from her
wind-ripped course,
lost, lurking
somewhere on the line
of tides
and ghosts like a fable
into our dreamtime.

Not fully here
below the drift of years,
a legend
never clearly seen,
somewhere at the edge,
sandhills of the Great
rolling Southern Ocean.
She comes about,
close-hauled, driven
hard before the storm
and rides the farthest
drifting beach
into our imagination.

2

This ship is built
of hard, dark wood,
her decks of softer stuff
eroded years ago
and here in a cleft
between the hummocks,
a spit of sand
where the Merri River lagoons,
its path blocked by sandhills,
west of Warrnambool,
Port Fairy further west,
lies below the sand,
sometimes only partly clear,
until the 1880s,
showing hulls, ribs
of deck and fo'c'sle,
remains of aftercastle,
surviving
planks of hard, red wood,
not teak or oak –
this is a wreck
of Iberian wood,
this old ship
so strangely built
of dark mahogany.

This wreck is not
clinker-built,
no overlapping wood
but planks that meet the seams
flush, after the fashion
of a panelled door
with mouldings stout and strong.
This ship's no galleon,
more lighter or a barge
with deep, capacious holds,
built for strength, endurance,
not for speed or size
and on the driest sandhills,
thirty feet above the bay
yet she has endured.

This is not a British,
nor in any way
a modern ship. The tribes
just smile and shrug and say
she's been there always,
this visitor
from the mind's confusion
of mist and fog,
this old ship
of strange
and dark mahogany.[1]

3

I, Christovão de Mendonça,
of the port of Lisbon,
in the reign of good King Sebastian,
this year, the seventy-fourth
of life, blinded now,
recount this to my only daughter,
Isabel, despite my oath
of strictest secrecy, sworn on pain
of slow and lingering death,
so many years ago –
what care I with death
in every nook and cranny and in every bay
of every voyage held in memory
and my maps, my charts, all my charts,
my logs and journals safely stowed
for future generations in the vaults,
secure in the cellars of the stout
House of India and the East,
in the royal Ribeiro Palace,
here in Lisbon on the banks
of the Tejo River.[2]
I say this for my daughter
who, also sworn to secrecy,
so too her sons so at my death
great voyages made in stealth,
achievements and the lore
of years ago, will not be lost
to common men and soon
my name will live.

4

We sailed from Ternate,
snug in the world's east,
the rich and far Moluccas, and steering
south the straight between Buru and Amboina,[3]
took a bearing west of Tanimbar,
tacked and stood away south-east,
January, the fourteenth day,
the year of our loved and blessed Lord
1521 and in darkest secret,
unknown but full aware, crossed
the treaty line of Tordesillas
into the Spanish world. Secret, secret
our voyage, our purpose and our discoveries,
three caravels, two hundred men,
my flagship *King Manuel*,
one hundred-thirty tons, her captain
hand-picked, my friend and colleague
Pedro Tavares, comrade in so many
battles against the heathen on land
and sea, brave, loyal, determined, fair.
My second ship, slightly smaller,
the *Blessed Mary,* her captain
new to me, selected by the governor
of Forte de Sao in Ternate, dark,
obsessive Juan Figuera, who rarely
spoke unless to give an order
and expected to be obeyed.

My smallest ship, some sixty tons,
the sprightly, shapely *Saint Anton*,
her captain Bart de Souza, mild
and stately like his ship, but confident
in his command and strangely fierce
in time of danger or in times of need.
Our orders twofold, first, but never
foremost, though sometimes foremost in my mind,
to intercept by stealth and kill
the hulking, warlike galleons
of Ferdinand Magellan, should we find him
anywhere he'd strayed west of the treaty line.
We know he'd fouled the far Pacific
and could be steering ever north
and west towards our spice-rich
empire in the Indies, so we
protect and nourish vital trade
in cinnamon, nutmeg, in cloves
and pepper, from the filthy hands
of Spain. What better place
to kill his ships than here,
the arse-end seas of Spanish empire
years to the west of God-knows-where,
but where he was and would we meet him
lay only in the hands of God.

Though more important, perhaps far more dangerous,
and far more secret, never announced
to anyone at all, on pain of death,
ourselves to cross the treaty line
that separates our western half the globe
from the Spanish east, our task of exploration
and diplomacy, within the world of Spain,
to prove the scholars right,
that the desert lands of nightmare,
Ouro, ironic name the Isles of Gold
our ships had hit sailing east from India[4]
but pushed off course miles to the south,
connect the landmass south of Java
with Antarctic wastes of rock and ice,
south of the wild Cape Deseado[5]
in one continuous and magic coast
of Greater Java, runs the straights
of John of Lisbon and is
the Great South Land, the Continent of Gold.
Damn Magellan who could trace
my magic coast from south to west
while I confined sailed north to east
but God forgive me, when I say
that what I found, explored and mapped –
Oh, what a waste of world!

5

We sighted soon the northern coast
of Ouro and hugged it east[6]
across the vast and ghostly gulf,[7]
an ocean in itself, of dreams
unknown hopes and fears, perhaps
the mouth of some huge river
flowing somewhere from the south.
We hit, as we were told we would,
the western tip and warped away
around the jungled landmass
of this unknown cape, the straights,
the islands, currents and the winds
against us. This is a shallow sea,
this treacherous Land of Waters.[8]

My ships, superb for exploration,
their fore-and-aft rigged lateen sails,
could head as close as ten degrees
against the wind, but here were reefs,
islands, narrow channels and tides.
We sometimes pulled our ships by small boat,
men at the oars and human muscle
to drag the ships along and always,
the *Saint Anton* ahead to weave
a passage. At length, we rounded safely
and looking east to see the coast
dipping gentle south by east, we gaped
instead, tropic, sparkling blue,
a vast and empty ocean
and realized that here, though not
perhaps for long, this new
and green and Spanish coast
traced directly south. What other
sharp surprises here in a world
so empty, strange and unexplored.

I considered this and asked opinion
of all my captains, Figuera
fixed me with determined stare and said,
'I'm lusting to explore the eastern sea.
The Land of Gold is east of here,'
Tavares and de Souza not so sure.
Tavares argued. 'This coast could be the northern
outskirts of the Great South Land, whose coasts
may dip and sway, but should proceed
mainly south and east.' De Souza agreed. 'Directly east
of here is empty ocean, islands perhaps, but open ocean.'
Figuera shouted that God had told him
and he knew there was land due east of here
and said no more as if his final word was spoken.

I considered this and partly to appease
his lust and partly to appease my own
impatience to explore, I ordered
we set course south and east, to hit, I hoped,
the coast again in some day's time
and drifted slowly far from land,
a risk worth taking as Magellan,
we prayed, should be as yet, half a world away.
And yes to my judgement, so the theories
of the learned proved my plan correct,
and in no less than seven days
to starboard rose the unknown coast
and in a far and gentle curve
of land, I named it Judgement Bay.
It met us always south by east,
a landmass we thought would lie across
the whole southern tip of globe, to balance
Asia and Europe in the north.

Veering eastward once again,
the coast now right across our track,
Thank God, a south-east wind, we tacked
and even turning north took easting past
a grand, imposing headland I named
Cape of King Manuel, and then
again the coast turned east of south,
direct towards the Great South Land.

My ships were small and easily handled
obedient to tiller and with little
change of sail direction, could cope
with adverse winds and hug the coast
where bigger ships, so cumbersome
and clumsy in the teeth of wave and wind,
must keep miles off shore.
What a coast! Green and savage jungle
crashed the blazing sands
and this grand ocean thundering there
in rollers and huge surf, even from
the furthest rich Americas perhaps.
Running parallel, a spine of ranges,
sometimes smoke, perhaps the hearth fires
of natives living there, a land so strange,
inhabited, though never harbour, dock
or quay, no towns or cities, farms or roads,
but fearing both their vessels and their laws,
we kept sharp lookout and kept our course
well within the sight of land,
as prudent we could dare and watched in awe
the jagged teeth of coral we knew lay
not far to port.

6

I thank my god for dear Magellan
for without that Spanish pig
to search for at the high crows' nest,
my sharpest hand-picked men for lookout,
ordered yell like mad at any sail
coming north to cross us or
pounding away from land to guard
their king's marine defences,
our three ships would be
drifting spar-wood on the sea
and every man a corpse. Reefs!
Coral reefs to port, ahead
breakers honing knife-edged pikes
and daggers to rip our ships
to shreds on an alien Spanish coast,
leagues to the east of anywhere
and death like a wolf kept snarling there.

We sheltered several weeks
in a river mouth, a clean[9]
protected harbour, watered, hunted there
the strangest, large and hopping mouse,
rested, drew our charts and records
of trees and plants, the animals
and even here the black, the lithe
and silent men, cousins to the gentle
creatures known to us in Greater Java,
uncivilised, naked, but not afraid.
We traded meat for coins and nails
and other specious junk they love.

On my orders only officers
to approach the natives, no weapons
to be carried, but open-handed we would put
trade goods on the ground, step back and indicate
for them to come. Confusion at first, but then
we pointed to our mouths and bellies
and they bought us meat, whole animals
they'd speared, whole fish, huge lizards, we cooked
on open fires. Also on my orders,
'No one to leave the camp.' I had
three men flagged until their backs were raw
for wandering into the bush and after that
no one dared. I could not afford to lose
a single man. I could not afford
to frighten or antagonise the natives,
everyone a future citizen of Spain
and any warlike act against them
war against the Spanish whose waters
we had trespassed on.

It was here the priest Father Christian
known as Gonsalves, his face black with fear
and prayer beads constantly entwined,
quietly said to me, 'We're damned, all of us
for being here. God will punish us.
We must return at once.' His eyes were wild,
his voice a plea. 'The Pope has divided
rightly all the world in half, the west for us,
the east for Spain, and we, we trespass here,
in lands forbidden to us, where the Pope
decreed, we should not be! We must return!
I fear my death by drowning but more I fear
my death at the hands of men.'

I was amazed. Gonsalves, the purist priest of God,
hand-picked as only one of six holy men
to guard our souls, hear confession, daily mass
and preach the love of God to any primitive
on this coast. 'Return?' I murmured, then said
'No way that. We carry out the will of God
in mapping here, the will of our king, and should
the Spanish ever fail and fail, dear God,
they must, this land is ours by right of clear
exploration.' I fixed my eyes on him.
'We must convert the natives to the one true faith
and the love of Christ.' I added only
as an afterthought, but in his eyes I saw
he did not believe me, then, 'Pray,
forgiveness of our sins and God will forgive us all,
our disobedience of the Pope, when all is said,
a man like us.' My words were not convincing
to myself, or him. I asked him why,
thinking as he did, he'd joined the expedition.
He glared at me 'I was ordered,'
all he said and walked away.

7

Calmly gliding out Mendonça Harbour,
south east a vicious reef, hidden
shark's-teeth coral, undersea
and only spotted by the sharpest eyes.[10]
By the grace of God so narrowly
averted that any other mariner
sailing north, the sun's glare
blinding in his eyes or shadowed, moonlit
night must rip his ship to pieces here
and may Magellan, if he gets this far,
take it in the teeth. I named this place
so rightly as Coast of Hidden Dangers.
We gave our thanks to God and named
the beach directly south our safe and glad
deliverance, holy Bay of Trinity.

It was then the words of the mad priest
rang in my head. Our ships tacked out
against a south-east breeze and all
was almost lost, but God had saved us.
I realised then I was right, Gonsalves was wrong.
I asked good Pedro what he knew
of Father Christian and why he was ordered
onto my ship. He looked at me and smiled,
'Rumours, rumours only, but he is said
to be intensely fond of little boys,'
and looked away and said no more.

My only order then, as I thought best,
Gonsalves, Father Christian, transferred
from my ship, *King Manuel*, to Figuera
on the *Blessed Mary*, and their priest, good
Father John, came to me. I thought Figuera's
lust to explore could soothe the guilt in him.
Alas, but I was wrong.

8

So forever, as it seemed, south-east,
Cedar Bay and Heron Island, Rocky Beach
and Broad Beach, Broad Sound, then to Mission Beach
where all our priests put ashore
to preach the gospel of Our Lord
to heathens who we sensed were there
but could not see, so light their steps,
so they preached to empty air.
Then past the Great Sandy Island,
Pebbly Beach and Four-Mile Beach,
Double Island, Green and Crescent Islands,
then False Cape and mapping, charting
on Palm Island, Cape Bowling Green and so
Bowling Green Bay, Hook Island, charting
mapping, navigating, one eye alert
for shoals and reefs, always in the east,
many a sharp-eyed danger on the coast
and eyes always for any sign of sail.
Broad Bay, Mount Tempest, Blue Lake Island,
Rainbow Beach, Seven Mile and then Pearl Bay.[11]
Yet strangely there, the line of latitude
South twenty-eight degrees, slow at first,
then faster, all began to slide away,
a slow turn west of south
and league on league and mile on mile
tracked away from the Land of Gold.

In conference, Figuera made his claim,
'This is not the Land of Gold – it lies
east and south, far into the broad Pacific.
This is wasteland, green and rich for sure
but here are only primitives. It belongs to Spain.
We cannot use it, there's nothing to take home,
Nothing to make us rich. Sail east and leave
This green land, continent of nothing.'

Tavares answered, 'We're only at latitude
twenty-eight. The southern land lies a world away.
This is a gulf or bay, the coast will shift
away from us and prove to be
our land of legend yet.'
Figuera flared, a man not used to contradiction,
'I say we sail directly east and find it now,'
and brought his first sharply down upon my table.
The three all looked at me, their admiral
for decision and Figuera's face told me
answer now, but de Souza said quietly,
'Our ships are small, built to hug the coast,
long ocean voyages are far beyond their strength.
I think it best to follow this coast
to where it leads us. This coast is God's
great gift to us, we cannot toss it in his face.'
I thanked him, smiled and said, 'Our men
are healthy, the ships strong, we've meat,
we've water, we've traced this coast for months,
we know what's here. It's time to widen
what we do. We'll sail south-east three weeks,
no more, and if all we find is sea, we'll
find this coast again and sail it to its end.'
This I thought a prudent compromise.
Figuera left my ship an angry man.

9

Pedro almost whispered as our ship *King Manuel*
changed course, her great lateen swung above our heads,
the steersmen gripped the tiller and the whole ship creaked
as both the smaller ships followed in our wake,
'Figuera's crazy but we'll need to see
this coast sweep east or he'll kill us all.
I see the lust for gold but also blood lust in his eyes.'
I asked good Pedro what he thought the best.
He said, 'Wait. Be patient. If all else fails,
we've found a new land and the Spanish haven't.
It could be ours, but wait, there could be more
and if there is, we'll find it.' Good Pedro
thanks be to God for your support and love.

We sailed away the east as far we could,
but nothing, only open sea, no shore,
no sign of shore, but ocean rollers
and deep swells. The twenty-second day
I hailed the *Blessed Mary* and the *Saint Anton*,
change course my order, south-west towards
the known coast of Greater Java. Figuera
launched his boat, charged and crashed against my hull,
said I was a fool to turn back now.
I took him free on board and almost yelled.
'We must go south, follow the land we know,
and when it turns as turn it must, east,
we'll find the land of gold?' Again Figuera
returned an angry man but I heard him
order across the sea, 'Go about, set course
south-west!' And then the scream from Father Christian.
'Go back, go north. Please God, let all of us
escape from here. God will punish us!' And
then I saw Figuera take him by the throat
and punch him hard, so he fell, and I saw no more.

10

We sailed away the west as far we could
and putting back a line of cliffs[12]
and then a bay, wide and open-mouthed.[13]
We anchored on the northern edge,
fresh water here and fish to put in store.
From upstream a small and fragile river.[14]
A flat and sheltered bay with southern shore
of sandhills and a larger river
emptied there in swamp and mangroves.[15]
All around low-lying land, sodden yet
a haven for the fish and gulls, for eels,
stingrays so rightly called Portugese Men of War,
and trees and flowers and bushes, herbs and shrubs.
My naturalists went mad with glee
so I named this bay for new-found science,
this Bay of Botany. The northern river
again we named for Blessed Mary, both
the mother of beloved Christ and Figuera's stately ship
and the southern river for my captain,
careful, patient, Pedro Tavares.

Then ever southwards, bays and rivers,
beaches, lakes and sandhills but west of south,
forever west, away from the Great South Land.
We passed a mountain on its side
like a camel so it was named in jest
Dromedary Hill. Then as always[16]
with the westing rainswept setting sun,
with sound advice from trusted captains,
cartographers and men of science,
as well my stout, my sound lieutenants
to put ashore, though not I ordered here,
this sweeping double bay, folded mid-placed
island, far too wide for larger safety
in an anchorage, too open to attack,
exposed to southern gales and prying eyes,
with cliffs around the south, no way
secure from our potential enemy.

11

In a small and nearly landlocked river mouth,[17]
some miles to the south of Twofold Bay,
we built a fort of local stone
with seashell mortar, stone-walled rooms
living quarters, kitchens and latrines.
We laboured hard and in two weeks
had walls and a wooden roof
to store our tools, our arms and seeds.

We planted corn and posted look-outs,
cliffs above who, sensitive to any sail,
daily spotted without fail pods of whales.
From here, at any hour, by stealth, make way,
out to force Magellan's blackened soul away
and keep our spice rich empire safe. We then
careened our ships, all three their foul and slimy keels,
stitched the square sails, spread lateens from masts and spars,
corked the hulls and decks, hunted, fished, explored
the forest, traded, slept with native women,
those whose men so wary sometimes offered.
But always there the nagging doubt – is this
the edge of the Great South Land? Then why
for love of dearest God, tends this coast
forever west? And why the swells,
the weather, wind and breezes, and the gales
come to us so often from the south, as if
south-east of here is nothing, only water.

For long and arduous council, meetings,
arguments and prayers for God's advice,
I asked, 'Should I split the expedition?'
Figuera at once replied, 'I should,'
and volunteered to take his ship away
to the east, while Tavares to my surprise
agreed, but de Souza, again to my surprise
launched a savage, bitter, personal attack
on Figuera and bought to public view
something we all had long suspected –
Figuera thought he should have been
admiral of the expedition, never me,
and all his disagreement built
on envy and the need for power. De Souza
saw the cunning in his eyes and cried,
'You can't be trusted, Captain Figuera –
even should you find the Land of Gold,
you'll not return, you'll claim it for yourself.'
Figuera slowly, darkly looked at him,
'Then trust me not, you pure and lily white,
go yourself and bring back bars of gold,
to prove you've found what every man here seeks
or don't come back at all.'
De Souza stood, 'I'll go. You stay here and rot!'

I took a vote, then made decision,
Figuera, de Souza, Tavares for,
myself in honest indecision
and thus I split the expedition
and sent, alas, the *Saint Anton*,
her captain brave Bartholemew de Souza
and with her fifty men, her crew,
to reconnoitre further east, the sea,
while the rest, some hundred-forty strong
enjoyed it here the mild, sweet, winter sun.
I issued strictest orders, 'Bart,
no matter what, return two months, no more!'
We waited there six months in all
and to my throat-tight stomached shame,
no one saw his ship again.

I stood on the beach alone
and stared at the empty sea
and cursed how the thin horizon line
brought nothing at all for me.

I stood in the forest alone
and listened to wind in the leaves
and writhed with light as the trees
refused their secrets to me.

I stood on the bend of the river
as its waters ran to the sea
and harnessed my thoughts to the ship
so the winds brought it safe to me.

I stood alone as the weeks rolled by,
as the days spun away with the sun
and choked and gasped that the wind-ripped sea
would deny its return to me.

12

Figuera's men, or most, were loyal to him.
They wanted gold. Tavares and his men,
loyal to me, as the camp dissolved,
two camps and then to our dismay,
to three. Gonsalves kept preaching, 'Return,
go back, we're dammed and bound to hell,'
and some men listened and many prayed with him.

Native women caused the first affray –
in innocence they offered themselves for nails,
for tools, for cloth, a trade I banned
and used the lash to skin the backs
of every man who stole our needed tools
to buy the body of a woman. The trade
soon stopped but then the rape and three men speared,
not killed but nasty wounds in thighs and legs
and so I banned the natives from our camp
and ordered the severest punishment
for anyone who wandered into the bush
fearing confrontation, violence, death.
Oh damn him to the deepest hell, Gonsalves
against my orders, took a dozen men
armed with muskets to find and shoot
the women. Like magic, like a silence
the natives melted into air. The forest
empty. He found none.

On his return, I told Figuera, 'Punish him.
He's your chaplain,' who merely locked him
in a cabin for a day and asked, 'How
do you punish a priest? With death?'
I wished I could have answered yes.
And then, Gonsalves refused the sacrament
to his captain, who, in rage and frenzy
sought the loyalty of Father John and Father Charles
who simply said, 'Avoid the man! He's mad
with guilt and sin. We'll talk and pray with him.'

I took Gonsalves back, second chaplain to the *King Manuel*
and spoke to wise Tavares, who advised,
'I'll separate the priest from his adherents.
I'll order him be quiet on pain of torture,'
It didn't work, night and day and every mass
he ranted against Figuera. 'He's the devil's
henchman, sent to lead us all into the pit,
the rising sun, the east is hell, Figuera's
spirit to the land of Satan.'
I threatened him with imprisonment. I locked him
in our store room built of stone. He yelled
and cursed so all the camp could hear.
I let him free, I tied him to a tree.
I let him free but under guard
to Pedro's great disgust. 'But what to do,'
I said to him, 'The men are nervous,
his influence grows and I do not trust Figuera.'

13

Six men punished for theft, all Figuera's crew.
He ordered each a hundred lashes
of the cat o'nines. I ordered
the whole expedition there to watch,
in a square, six barebacked thieves strapped to trees.
The miscreants writhed and screamed
as the whips took off their skin. Gonsalves watched,
launched himself at Figuera's throat.
'Devil's whore, what right to punish
men who know the voyage doomed and act
as if it's doomed right now.' I stepped
towards him, 'Damn you, priest. Your captain has
the right to punish criminals and I gave him
my permission,' and to the sergeants
with all their red lashes hanging in their hands,
'Carry on, do your duty. Another twenty
lashes for each man!' Figuera, bigger,
stronger than the priest threw him off and down
and kicked him. Goncalves stalked away,
then ran into the bush. I ordered
his arrest. Four marshals followed him.
The miscreants suffered another drawn-out
fifty lashes and screamed and pleaded
as they writhed and bled. The hissing
of cords through air and the thud of each
on flesh, the noise of six men screaming
for the love of God, but all heads turned
when my four men returned, the body
of the priest hanging limp, half his head
shot away, and Figuera still
and white but standing in a different place.

Tavares was loudest in his condemnation,
'Arrest him, imprison him, torture him.
Force him to confess,' but then I said,
'No one saw him leave, no one saw him return,
no one saw him kill the priest, no one heard
a thing above the crying of those wretches.'
'You mean you think he didn't do it?'
Pedro looked at me amazed. 'No,' I said,
'there are twenty, thirty, more, who wished him dead,
but if he did it, the priest was mad, he
might have done us all a favour,
or not have done it with his own hand
but issued orders for the priest to die,
or was a pistol left from that imbecile
expedition to murder all the women
and Gonsalves used it on himself.'
But no pistol was ever found near his body.
'Figuera's mad. I told you he had
blood lust in his eyes. Abandon him here.
Let him seek his gold among the savages.'

I could not replace a seaman good as him
so I left Figuera in his place, captain
of the *Blessed Mary*, but never spoke
a word direct to him again.
I questioned every man, Pedro questioned
Figuera himself, no one saw or heard a thing
and what happened to the pistol,
we never knew but only later half-suspected.
On the *King Manuel* only Pedro,
captain of my flagship, friend, advisor,
ever spoke again direct to Figuera
and no one of our crew.

I named this place so happy
and so sad, Decision Bay
and the small fresh water stream
Port de Souza and the next cape south
so green and fresh, Saint Anton's Head.[18]
The rock toothed, threatening and wind-swept bay
waiting south beyond the cliffs
is now sad Disaster Bay.

14

Leaving stores and food and heartfelt prayers
for safe return of Saint Anton her crew,
we made departure and set sail,
a sad departing putting out to sea
but two ships left of three,
I took the *King Manuel* and the sturdy
Blessed Mary down the Cape of Flowers
and then, for dear Christ's sake I cannot
tolerate the thought today, around that cursed,
hollow line of the southern latitude
at thirty-eight, we passed so grand,
magnificent a cape, I named Fremose,[19]
but there the coast, Lord and one and only Saviour,
there the coast turned and ran directly west.
We knew from that true bearing then
Magellan would not come. But in his place,
from the west confused and vicious
seas, sometimes calm but often armed
like Saracens with westerlies.
Shallow water off this shipwreck coast
and this I fear is not the Land of Gold
for Portugal, for Spain and nor, alas, for me.

Though here the largest harbour seen.
Its heads behind an eastern narrow cape
and welcoming the west, we braced
a strong and inwards current here and logged
an empty bay so wide, a mountain
rounded east, the other shore unseen.[20]
A northern river, smaller, less majestic
but I so homesick named it after Lisbon's,[21]
New Tagus and this King Manuel's Gulf.
Though flat and nondescript the land,
the west a plain much like but larger here
than the northern Bay of Botany,
I claimed this land and all we'd found
and damned to Spain, I called it yet New Portugal.
We anchored in a smaller gulf the west
and named it Gulf of Caravels.[22]
So sad that not a single name
ever set on this new and empty land
would ever live outside my maps
as then by treaty, sound bilateral
diplomacy and law, we knew all lay
so starkly east of the treaty line
Tordesillas, all in the Spanish
half of the world. But, Isobel, now I know
beyond a doubt, no Spaniards
ever set foot here and we, only we,
Mendonça and my caravels, had traced
and mapped the very first of anyone
this green and richest virgin coast.

So all one hundred of my men,
as much myself sworn to firmest
secrecy on everything we saw or
would forever see, lest word spring out
to fascist Spain, another noble empire lies
across our empire's southern throat.
And here more wonders to relate.
By signs and gestures, grunts and single words,
we just deciphered native tales
that meant, not many generations past
perhaps, all this shallow, harbour sound,
new King Manuel's Gulf had been
once dry land, where streams and rivers ran
and blackmen wandered, hunted, stalked
their food, which now we sail upon
and this they said, I think they said,
or something like, was not so long ago.

And then the matter of the keys. Figuera
told Tavares who reported it to me,
a set of keys, the lock to the captain's
pistol cabinet, lost, missing
from his cabin. His steward and two boys
tortured but did not know, or would not tell,
how the keys were lost. Figuera interviewed
again each man but nothing. 'Damn him,'
Pedro hissed, 'the pistol he used
to murder the mad priest is in that locker,
now he'll say he can never show it.
He probably threw his keys away[23]
somewhere in the bay.' I ordered
a carpenter on the *Blessed Mary*
to break the lock, Figuera's status
as his captain notwithstanding.
I ordered every gun, both ships
to be accessed in case sudden attack,
for self-defence. Pedro's locker
carried twelve, Figuera's only eleven.
'He's hidden the other somewhere
on his ship or left it in the place he
murdered the priest.' I let the matter lapse,
as Figuera swore he knew of no missing gun.

15

On gliding out King Manuel's Gulf
we tracked a wild and mountainous coast
where hills and valleys fought to tumble
onto waves and beaches, till rounding
the Cape of Terra Alta there, we knew[24]
and every sailor sensed, each officer and crew
just stopped his work and stared because he knew,
the long and rolling swells, sweeping like a world
from south and west, this coast began to drift
away the north and from ahead
vast and empty open ocean
as far perhaps the greatest Cape Good Hope,
the land we'd tracked the last two years,
its coasts so vast and massive, all so wide,
they knew, this land indeed, an island.

One last and fateful judgement made,
we'd move due west then steering north
pick up again the coast of desert Ouro
and circumnavigating then this Greater Java
return to Ternate with news
both sombre and amazing – that we'd found
a southern continent but not
alas the fabled continent of gold.
This realm must lie much further south and east,
as Figuera said, if it exists at all.

So tracking west against the swell,
with sea room to spare along the gales,
a blackened sky, an icy wind, rain and squalls
and this no placid, tropic, turquoise sea.
We faced ferocious crests and beat
south west as far we could
away the Highland Coast – with topsail
and after mizzen storm-sail set to steer
and nothing else, and great lateens we clewed away,
as seas like jaws and waves like teeth
and spits of wind sliced like sabres
and cutlesses out of the west and south. We faced
pure hell afloat. Our caravels were driven logs
and all thanked God for sturdy seamed and stout
construction and the good, hard Lisbon planks
our shipwrights had the skill to build in them.
With sea room vast for leagues around
we knew we'd run before the storm
and pounded hard we thought due west
away from the shipwreck coasts.

But Satan's teeth
defined in black and blind with salt despair,
we lost the *Blessed Mary* there.
Running helpless, tempest-diced, black currents surged
and shuttered, driving her to port of us
onto a low lee shore and with devil's blasts,
frantic those with will to live, to bring her
safely out, not here the Highland Coast we feared
but surf crashed, death itself and sand dunes
fierce ahead, ran full tilt inshore and split
her backbone on a ridge of grim-cursed,
ship-break, God-lost damned and foul this coast,
of sandhills grey against the sea.

We kept, thanks only Blessed Lord,
the *King Manuel* far out to sea
and almost fetched ourselves ashore
on the rock-nailed coast of yet another,
outer devil's island – we saved frantic,[25]
but only just, the ship and all our lives.
We crawled and tacked like sodden cats
against a falling sea-surge wind to find
the *Blessed Mary*, until we picked her wreck
midway, shelved in a shallow, sandy bay
and wind abating set ashore our small boats there.

Of once her sixty men we found alive
just twenty-two and some more dead
than living. Her captain, Juan Figuera,
his body was never found.

A week we lay so far off shore
and stripped the wreck, her stores not sodden
or water-spoiled, loose timber, rope, her pitch and spars,
sailcloth – all we salvaged from the wreck
then slowly, sadly turned back east,
not risking once again our ship
on the devil's southern ocean,
one ship of three to haul our maps,
our sketches, specimens and most our lives
back to the secrecy of home.

16

I, Christovão de Mendonça
now in the port of Lisbon,
safe at home in Portugal,
in the reign of King Sebastian,
blind and close to death,
relate these words, that fifty men
of our two hundred, limped back home to Ternate.
I give thanks to God above all else
I saved all my precious maps.
I'm sworn on pain of death to guard
my secret, all so close and well. No one
could ever know the fate of the *Saint Anton*,
dear Bart and all his crew. Remains there
the *Blessed Mary* smashed beyond repairs –
could still be there these forty years
wrecked on the sand-cursed, devil's coast,
the island continent of Greater Java,
I mapped in 1523, with the graves
of most her men.

17

Somewhere at the edge
sandhills of the great
rolling Southern Ocean,
close-hauled and driven,
this ancient, secret ship,
this ship of dark mahogany,
rides the farthest
drifting beach
of our imagination
and lurks there still,
half buried here
beneath the modern metres
of what was Spanish
and is now
Australian sand.

Christovão de Mendonça
Lisbon, 1564.

Notes

Reference: Kenneth Gordon McIntyre (1977), *The Secret Discovery of Australia: Portugese ventures 200 years before Captain Cook*. Souvenir Press, Adelaide.

1. The Mahogany Ship was a wreck of antique and strange appearance almost entirely buried in the sand dunes, about halfway between modern Warnambool and Port Fairy, in Victoria, seen by about twenty-seven people between 1836 and 1880. It has not been seen since but is reported to have been built of dark redwood, with the characteristics of Portugese oak and to have planks meeting flush at the seams, like a caravel.

2. Totally destroyed with all its contents in the great Lisbon earthquake of 1755, the flooding and fires which followed.

3. It is known that a fleet of three caravels under Cristovão de Mendonça sailed in 1521 with orders to search the Isles of Gold, probably for Magellan. Where he went, when or if he returned is not known to history and so the following account is totally fictional.

4. It is quite possible the Portugese explored and mapped the coasts of Australia 250 years before Cook, but little real evidence remains. Ouro is north-west Western Australia.

5. Cape Horn.

6. Arnhem Land.

7. The Gulf of Carpentaria.

8. Torres Strait.

9. Endeavour River, Cooktown.

10. Endeavour Reef, which almost destroyed Cook's *Endeavour*. He took refuge at Endeavour River, the site of modern Cooktown.

11. As many of these geographical features have names which reflect their appearance, I have used the names given by Cook

and Flinders, names that Mendonça might also have given them.

12. South of modern Sydney Harbour.

13. Botany Bay.

14. Cook's River.

15. Georges River.

16. Mount Dromedary, near Bermagui, NSW.

17. Bittangabee Bay, where the foundations of an old stone building still exist.

18. Green Cape.

19. Point Hicks.

20. Port Phillip Bay.

21. Yarra River.

22. Corio Bay.

23. A set of five corroded keys were discovered in 1847 at Limeburners Point, Corio Bay, near Geelong, in an excavation for lime, at about the old high-water level.

24. Cape Otway.

25. King Island.

www.ingramcontent.com/pod-product-compliance
Lightning Source LLC
Chambersburg PA
CBHW062204100526
44589CB00014B/1953